YOUR BIRTHDAY BOOK

a keepsake journal

by amy k.

potter style

Copyright © 2007 by Amy Krouse Rosenthal

All rights reserved.

Published in the United States by Clarkson Potter/Publishers,

an imprint of the Crown Publishing Group,

a division of Random House, Inc., New York.

Potter Style is a trademark and Potter and colophon are

registered trademarks of Random House, Inc.

ISBN 978-0-307-34230-0

Printed in China

Cover design by Jim Massey

Interior design by Jan Derevjanik

20 19 18 17 16 15 14 13 12

an introduction to
your
birthday book

Welcome to the moment where it all begins.

You and your child are about to embark on a magnificent lifelong journey. We hope this journal will prove to be one your most treasured, trusted, and lively companions.

A few tips (of the birthday candle) that might shed a little light on how you can fill out this book . . .

As you've probably already gathered, this is not anything like a baby book. It's also not a scrapbook. It's, well, a birthday book. It was born from the simple idea that birthdays provide the perfect opportunity to preserve a sweet moment in time and to check in with your child in a special and natural way. So it's a multilayered confection: annual touchstone, cherished ritual, and eternal keepsake.

Everything contained herein is meant to be fun, quick, and casual. There are plenty of things out there that fit the bill of complicated, time consuming, and obligatory—we sure hope this isn't one of them. Feel free to alter or skip over questions/sections if it's ever feeling like the latter. We want you and your child to look forward to this each year, not dread it.

Whether you come in at day one or year nine, whether you return to it like clockwork or end up skipping a year or two, it just doesn't matter. Even a half-filled-out journal will be an incredible gift to your child years from now.

The journal is flexible, malleable, structured to evolve with you and your child. In the early, prereading/writing years, you will undoubtedly steer the way. Later, you might fill it out together, tag-team style. And later still, your child/teen/young adult may choose to do sections entirely on his or her own.

From toddler hood to young adulthood to every 'hood in between, you'll return to the same four activities. The questions, prompts, and tone may shift slightly each year, but the essence intentionally remains in tact.

Snapshot Page ▪ A place to stick birthday photos and jot down a few "stats" about your kid (current best friends, funny thing he or she said lately).

Exclusive Interview ▪ This is truly the heart and soul of the journal. We've provided a series of alternately fun and thought-provoking questions to ask your child (and space for writing down the answers). See how he or she changes—and stays exactly the same—through the years.

Bonus Activity ▪ Some years it's something your child will do alone; some years it involves an outside participant (you can invite grandparents, siblings, and other relatives to contribute); but always, it's a playful exercise.

Time Capsule Envelope ▪ Stash away seemingly unimportant stuff, odds and ends, and small everyday nothings—all of which have a way of taking on heightened meaning and sentimentality over time.

So that's the scoop.

Now before you begin, close your eyes, take a deep breath, and make a wish . . .

Happy Birthday Book!

1 one-derful you

[photo here]

2 here's two you

[photo here]

3 three cheers

[photo here]

party
pictures: years
1, 2, & 3

[photo here]

[photo here]

[photo here]

1st BIRTHDAY

Your Big Day

Your very first birthday cake ever was _____.

Here's what you thought of it and how you ate it: _____

_____

_____

Family and friends who were there to celebrate with you include: _____

_____

_____

_____

Your favorite gift was: _____

_____

_____

Actually, what you most liked was:

⬤ the wrapping paper   ⬤ the box

Quick mental snapshot: When I close my eyes, this is how I picture you: _____

_____

_____

_____

_____

Your nicknames these days are _____.

_____ is your bestest little playmate.

You're really into _____ right now.

2nd BIRTHDAY

Your Big Day

You had a _____ themed party.

These were some of the dear family and friends who were there: _____
_____
_____

Your noisiest gift was _____ from
_____ (thanks for that!)

Your guests received a goody bag filled with _____
_____.

Quick mental snapshot: When I close my eyes, this is how I picture you: _____
_____
_____
_____
_____
_____
_____ is your bestest little buddy.

You're really into _____
_____ right now.

Funny thing YOU said recently . . .

3rd BIRTHDAY

Your Big Day

You had a _____ themed party.

Here's who was there: _____

_____

_____

Your cake was _____.

Your guests received a goody bag filled with _____

_____.

The highlight of the party was _____

_____.

Quick mental snapshot: When I close my eyes, this is how I picture you: _____

_____

_____

_____

Your nicknames these days are _____.

_____ is your best pal.

You're really into _____

_____ lately.

Funny thing YOU said recently . . .

exclusive
INTERVIEW

Conducted by _____.

I met with _____ on _____
            (CHILD'S NAME)   (DATE)

at our favorite spot, _____. My subject was dashing in

_____ and appeared quite _____
(ITEM OF CLOTHING WORN AT TIME)   (INTERESTED? BORED? HUNGRY?)

throughout the interview. We spoke on the record for about _____ minutes.

What were some of your favorite birthday gifts this year? _____

_____

_____

Tell me what you think of when I say these words:

Home _____ Favorite color _____

Brother/sister _____ Love _____

What's the last thing you were sad about? _____

_____

What makes you really *really* happy? _____

_____

_____

Are you scared of anything? _____

_____

What do you think you'd like to be when you grow up? _____

_____

Who's the last person you kissed? _____

Your signature: _____

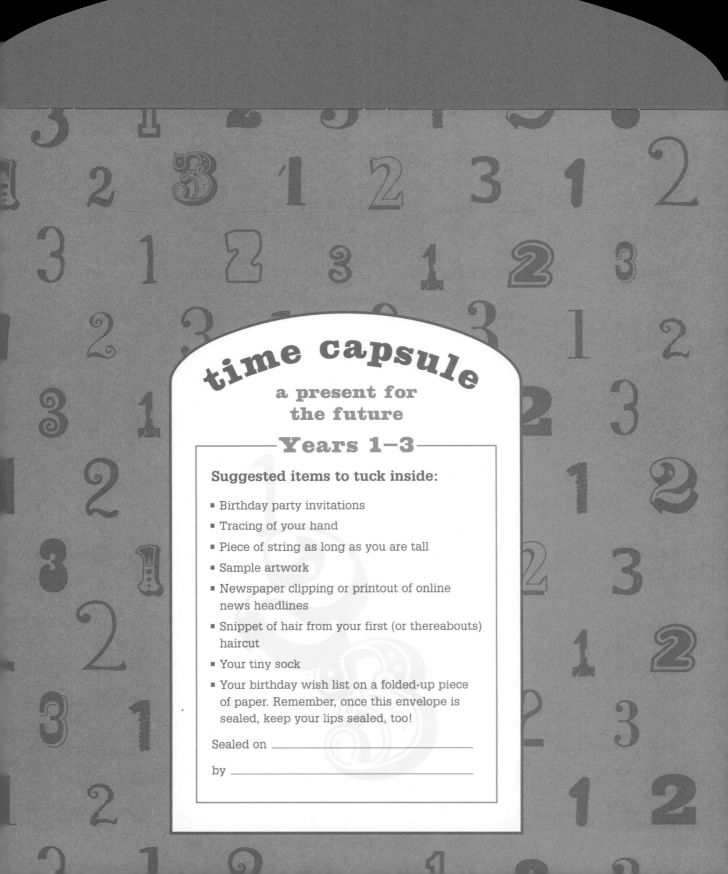

time capsule
a present for the future

Years 1–3

Suggested items to tuck inside:

- Birthday party invitations
- Tracing of your hand
- Piece of string as long as you are tall
- Sample artwork
- Newspaper clipping or printout of online news headlines
- Snippet of hair from your first (or thereabouts) haircut
- Your tiny sock
- Your birthday wish list on a folded-up piece of paper. Remember, once this envelope is sealed, keep your lips sealed, too!

Sealed on _____

by _____

4

fab-four

Random pic from your
4th year on earth

th BIRTHDAY

Your Big Day

You had a _____ themed party.

Some of the friends who celebrated with you: _____

_____

_____

Your cake was _____.

Your guests received a goody bag filled with: _____

_____

A highlight of the party was: _____

_____

_____

Quick mental snapshot: When I close my eyes, this is how I picture you: _____

_____

_____

Your current nicknames are _____.

_____ are your best pals.

You're really into _____ right now.

Funny thing YOU said recently . . .

exclusive
INTERVIEW

Conducted by _____.

I met with _____ on _____

(CHILD'S NAME)   (DATE)

at our favorite spot, _____. My subject was dashing in

_____ and appeared quite _____

(ITEM OF CLOTHING WORN AT TIME)   (INTERESTED? BORED? HUNGRY?)

throughout the interview. We spoke on the record for about _____ minutes.

What were some of your favorite gifts that you got this year? _____

Tell me what immediately comes to mind when I say these words:

Home _____ Favorite color _____ Brother/sister _____

Magic _____ Bedtime _____ School _____ Love _____

What's the last thing you were sad about? _____

_____

What makes you really *really* happy? _____

_____

Are you scared of anything? _____

_____

If you could have any animal in the world as a pet, what would it be? _____

_____

What do you think you'd like to be when you grow up? _____

_____

Do you like your name? _____

Who's the last person you kissed? _____

_____

Your signature: _____

big
thoughts
from a little person

At what age is a person officially a grown-up? _____

_____

_____

_____

_____

What does mom or dad do at work all day? _____

_____

_____

_____

_____

If you could always get everything that you want, do you think you'd always be happy? _____

_____

_____

_____

_____

What do you think heaven is like? _____

_____

_____

_____

_____

time capsule

a present for the future

——— Year 4 ———

Suggested items to tuck inside:

- Fourth birthday party invitation
- Tracing of your hand
- Piece of string as long as you are tall
- Sample artwork
- Newspaper clipping or printout of online news headlines
- Favorite candy wrapper
- Pre-school name tag, report card, or any other document from school
- Your birthday wish list on a folded-up piece of paper. Remember, once this envelope is sealed, keep your lips sealed, too!

Sealed on _____

by _____

5

high five! you're 5!

Random pic from your
5th year on earth

Your Big Day

You had a _____ themed party.

These were some of the friends who celebrated with you: _____
_____
_____

Your cake was _____.

Your guests received a goody bag filled with: _____
_____

A highlight of your party was: _____
_____
_____

Quick mental snapshot: When I close my eyes, this is how I picture you: _____
_____
_____

Your nicknames right now are _____.
_____ are your best pals.

You're really into _____.

Funny thing YOU said recently . . .

exclusive
INTERVIEW

Conducted by _____.

I met with _____ on _____
                    (CHILD'S NAME)   (DATE)

at our favorite spot,_____. My subject was dashing in

_____ and appeared quite _____
         (ITEM OF CLOTHING WORN AT TIME)   (INTERESTED? BORED? HUNGRY?)

throughout the interview. We spoke on the record for about _____ minutes.

What were some of your favorite gifts that you got this year? _____

Tell me what immediately comes to mind when I say these words:

Home _____ Favorite color _____ Brother/sister _____

Magic _____ Bedtime _____ School _____ Love _____

Besides your birthday, what is your favorite day of the year? _____

What's the last thing you were sad about? _____

What makes you really *really* happy? _____

What are your thoughts about God? _____

_____

What's your favorite thing to wear? How come? _____

_____

Now that you're five, is there any "big kid" thing you'd like to learn how to do? _____

_____

What do you think you'd like to be when you grow up? _____

_____

Who's the last person you kissed? _____

_____

Your signature: _____

_____'S

BIRTHDAY CAKE RECIPE

What are the ingredients in your cake? _____
_____
_____
_____

How do you combine them together? _____
_____
_____
_____

How long do you bake it in the oven? What temperature? _____
_____
_____
_____

What do you decorate the cake with? _____
_____
_____
_____

How many people does your cake serve? _____
_____
_____
_____

NOTE TO PARENT: Ask your kid to invent a cake recipe using all the yummy ingredients he or she can think of. The instructions will undoubtedly yield a pretty interesting birthday treat.

time capsule

a present for the future

— Year 5 —

Suggested items to tuck inside:

- Fifth birthday party invitation
- Tracing of your hand
- Piece of string as long as you are tall
- Sample artwork
- Newspaper clipping or printout of online news headlines
- A card that you made
- Certificate or award
- Your birthday wish list on a folded-up piece of paper. Remember, once this envelope is sealed, keep your lips sealed, too!

Sealed on _____

by _____

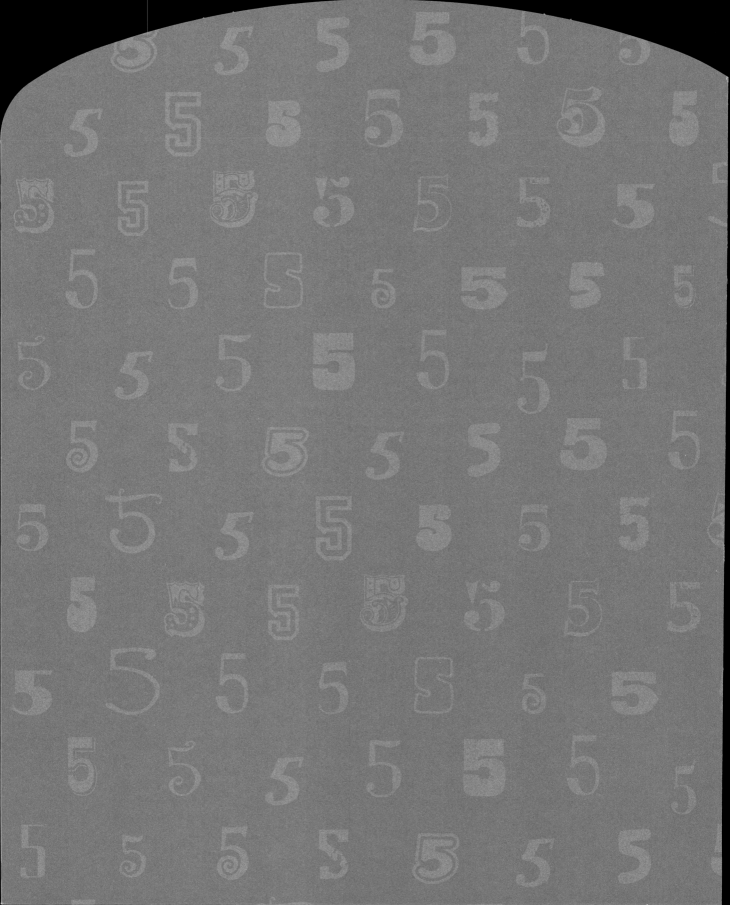

6

why is 6 scared of 7? because 7 ate 9.
you're 6, and that is no joke.

Random pic from your
6th year on earth

6th BIRTHDAY

· · · · · · · · · · · · · · · · · **Your Big Day** · · · · · · · · · · · · · · · ·

You had a _____ themed party.

These were some of the friends who joined you: _____

_____

_____

Your cake was _____.

Your guests received a goody bag filled with: _____

_____

A highlight of your party was: _____

_____

_____

Quick mental snapshot: When I close my eyes, this is how I picture you: _____

_____

_____

Your nicknames right now are _____.

_____ are your best pals.

You're really into _____.

Funny thing YOU said recently . . .

exclusive
INTERVIEW

Conducted by _____.

I met with _____ on _____
(CHILD'S NAME)   (DATE)

at our favorite spot,_____. My subject was dashing in

_____ and appeared quite _____
(ITEM OF CLOTHING WORN AT TIME)   (INTERESTED? BORED? HUNGRY?)

throughout the interview. We spoke on the record for about _____ minutes.

What were some of your favorite gifts that you got this year? _____

Tell me what immediately comes to mind when I say these words:

Home _____ Favorite color _____ Brother/sister _____

Magic _____ Bedtime _____ School _____

Hero _____ Love _____

What's the last thing you were sad about? _____

What makes you really *really* happy? _____

What do you look for in a friend? _____

Are you scared of anything? _____

So, what's it like to be losing all of those teeth? _____

_____

What do you like to do on Saturday mornings? _____

_____

What do you think you'd like to be when you grow up? _____

Besides your birthday, what is your favorite day of the year? _____

Who's the last person you kissed? _____

Your signature: _____

kid $ CURRENCY

bonus page

How much does the family car cost? _____

_____

_____

_____

Who is the biggest person you know? How tall do you think he or she is? How much does he or she weigh?

_____

_____

_____

Who is the littlest person you know? How tall do you think he or she is? How much does he or she weigh?

_____

_____

_____

If you were given a twenty dollar shopping spree at your favorite store, what could you buy? _____

_____

_____

_____

How many people do you think live in our neighborhood? How many live in the world? _____

_____

_____

_____

_____

NOTE TO PARENT: These questions are intended to capture your child's perception of the scale and value of everyday objects based on his or her current knowledge of the world.

time capsule

a present for the future

—— Year 6 ——

Suggested items to tuck inside:

- Sixth birthday party invitation
- Tracing of your hand
- Piece of string as long as you are tall
- Sample artwork
- Newspaper clipping or printout of online news headlines
- A card that you made
- Sample of first-grade homework
- First lost tooth and/or note from the tooth fairy
- Your birthday wish list on a folded-up piece of paper. Remember, once this envelope is sealed, keep you lips sealed, too!

Sealed on _____

by _____

7

lucky 7

Random pic from your
7th year on earth

7th BIRTHDAY

················ **Your Big Day** ················

You had a _____ themed party.

Your honored guests were: _____
_____
_____

Your cake was _____.

Your guests received a goody bag filled with: _____
_____

A highlight of your party was: _____
_____
_____

Quick mental snapshot: When I close my eyes, this is how I picture you: _____
_____
_____

We've started calling you _____.

You and _____ are inseparable right now.

You're really into _____.

Funny thing **YOU** said **recently . . .**

exclusive
INTERVIEW

Conducted by _____.

I met with _____ on _____
(CHILD'S NAME)   (DATE)

at our favorite spot, _____. My subject was dashing in

_____ and appeared quite _____
(ITEM OF CLOTHING WORN AT TIME)   (INTERESTED? BORED? HUNGRY?)

throughout the interview. We spoke on the record for about _____ minutes.

What were some of your favorite gifts that you got this year? _____

Tell me what immediately comes to mind when I say these words:

Home _____   Favorite color _____   Brother/sister _____

Magic _____   Bedtime _____   School _____

Hero _____   Cool _____   Love _____

What's the last thing you were sad about? _____

What makes you really *really* happy? _____

Now that you're seven, are there any new things you'd like to learn how to do? _____

_____

How do you like learning to read so far? _____

_____

How many teeth have you lost at this point? Do you like the replacements? _____

What do you think you'd like to be when you grow up? _____

Do you like your name? _____

Besides your birthday, what is your favorite day of the year? _____

Who's the last person you kissed? _____

Your signature: _____

we interrupt your regularly scheduled birthday for this

SPECIAL MESSAGE

My Dearest _____ ,

I'm so honored to be your _____ .

This is what I remember most about being your age: _____

_____

_____

_____

_____

If I could give you one piece of advice, it would be this: _____

_____

_____

_____

_____

If I could give you one piece of cake, it would be this, my most favorite kind: _____

_____

_____

May your seventh year bring you joy, _____ , and _____ .

Love, _____

time capsule

a present for the future

— Year 7 —

Suggested items to tuck inside:

- Seventh birthday party invitation
- Tracing of your hand
- Piece of string as long as you are tall
- Sample artwork
- Newspaper clipping or printout of online news headlines
- A card that you made or received
- Printout of an e-mail you wrote or received
- Program from a school recital or play
- Your birthday wish list on a folded-up piece of paper. Remember, once this envelope is sealed, keep your lips sealed, too!

Sealed on _____

by _____

8

super great-you are 8

Random pic from your
8th year on earth

8th BIRTHDAY

Your Big Day

You had a _____ themed party.

Your guest list included: _____

_____

_____

Your cake was _____.

Your guests were favored with: _____

_____

_____

A highlight of your party was: _____

_____

_____

Quick mental snapshot: When I close my eyes, this is how I picture you: _____

_____

_____

Your nicknames are _____.

_____ are your best pals.

You're really into _____.

Funny thing YOU said recently . . .

exclusive
INTERVIEW

Conducted by _____.

I met with _____ on _____
                  (CHILD'S NAME)   (DATE)

at our favorite spot, _____. My subject was dashing in

_____ and appeared quite _____
          (ITEM OF CLOTHING WORN AT TIME)   (INTERESTED? BORED? HUNGRY?)

throughout the interview. We spoke on the record for about _____ minutes.

What were some of your favorite gifts that you got this year? _____

Tell me what immediately comes to mind when I say these words:

Home _____ Favorite color _____ Brother/sister _____

Magic _____ Bedtime _____ School _____

Hero _____ Cool _____ Love _____

What's the last thing you were sad about? _____

What makes you really *really* happy? _____

What do you look for in a friend? _____

_____

What's the best way to cheer someone up? _____

_____

What's your favorite song on the radio? _____

What are your thoughts about God? _____

_____

What do you think you'd like to be when you grow up? _____

Who's the last person you kissed? _____

Your signature: _____

SLICE OF life

This is what we call a pie chart. Fill in the slices with the things in your life (school, friends, TV, sports, hobbies) according to their significance to you. Big slices are for the things that are most important to you or that you spend the most time doing, and little slices are for the less important, less time-consuming stuff. You can add more wedges if you'd like.

time capsule

a present for
the future

— Year 8 —

Suggested items to tuck inside:

- Eighth birthday party invitation
- Tracing of your hand
- Piece of string as long as you are tall
- Sample artwork
- Newspaper clipping or printout of online news headlines
- Letter that you sent from camp
- Report card or program from a school recital or play
- Random item from your room, coat pocket, or backpack
- Your birthday wish list on a folded-up piece of paper

Sealed on _____

by _____

9

9 years down, 9 more to go.
has it gone quickly? or has it gone slow?

Random pic from your
9th year on earth

9th **BIRTHDAY**

······················· **Your Big Day** ·······················

You had a _____ themed party.

Your guest list included: _____

_____

_____

Your cake was _____

Your guests were favored with: _____

_____

A highlight of your party was: _____

_____

_____

Quick mental snapshot: When I close my eyes, this is how I picture you: _____

_____

_____

Your nicknames are _____

_____ are your best pals.

You're really into _____

Funny thing **YOU** said **recently . . .**

exclusive
INTERVIEW

Conducted by _____.

I met with _____ on _____
_(CHILD'S NAME) _(DATE)

at our favorite spot,_____. My subject was dashing in

_____ and appeared quite _____
_(ITEM OF CLOTHING WORN AT TIME) _(INTERESTED? BORED? HUNGRY?)

throughout the interview. We spoke on the record for about _____ minutes.

What were some of your favorite gifts that you got this year? _____

Tell me what immediately comes to mind when I say these words:

Home _____ Favorite color _____ Brother/sister _____

Magic _____ Bedtime _____ School _____

Hero _____ Cool _____ Love _____

What's the last thing you were sad about? _____

What makes you really *really* happy? _____

What is your favorite piece of clothing? How come? _____
_____

If you could travel back in time, where would you go? _____
_____

If you could choose one super-human attribute, what would it be? _____
_____

What do you think you'd like to be when you grow up? _____

We're halfway through this book. What do you think of that? _____

Who's the last person you kissed? _____

Your signature: _____

bonus page

what was cool then . . . and now

grown-up side   **kid side**

Back in _____ **when I was 9 . . .**   **Right now in** _____

My favorite song was: My favorite song is:

_____   _____

My favorite movie was: My favorite movie is:

_____   _____

My favorite TV show was: My favorite TV show is:

_____   _____

My favorite book was: My favorite book is:

_____   _____

My favorite junk food was: My favorite junk food is:

_____   _____

My hero was: My hero is:

_____   _____

My friends and I collected: My friends and I collect:

_____   _____

It was cool to wear: It's cool to wear:

_____   _____

It was pretty dorky to wear: You're pretty dorky if you wear:

_____   _____

After school I would usually: After school I usually:

_____   _____

We listened to music on a: I listen to music on a:

_____   _____

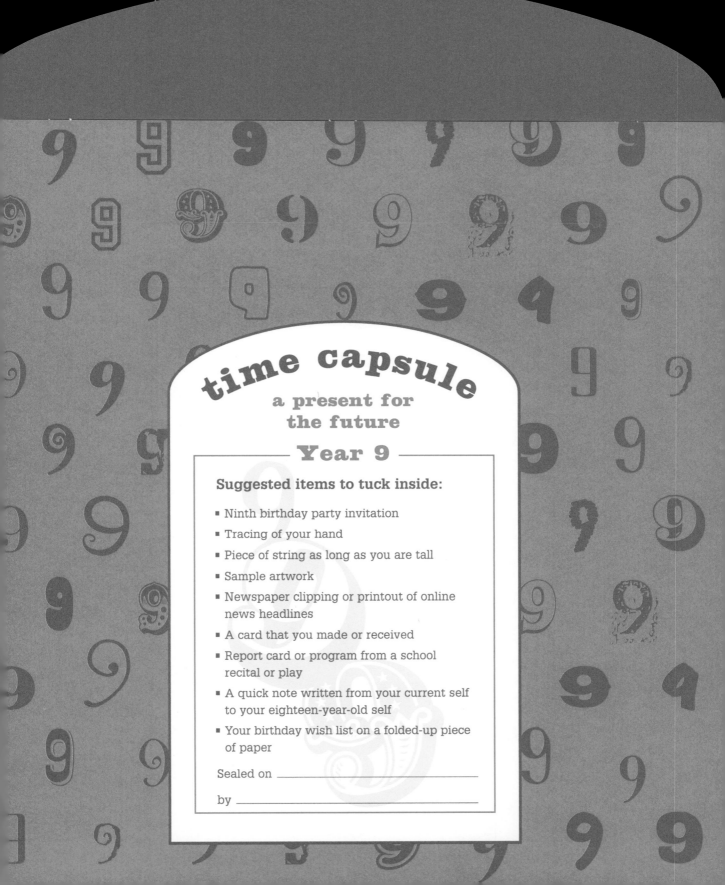

time capsule
a present for the future

Year 9

Suggested items to tuck inside:

- Ninth birthday party invitation
- Tracing of your hand
- Piece of string as long as you are tall
- Sample artwork
- Newspaper clipping or printout of online news headlines
- A card that you made or received
- Report card or program from a school recital or play
- A quick note written from your current self to your eighteen-year-old self
- Your birthday wish list on a folded-up piece of paper

Sealed on _____

by _____

10

Random pic from your
10th year on earth

10th BIRTHDAY

Your Big Day

You wanted to celebrate this landmark birthday by: _____

These were some of the friends who celebrated with you: _____

_____

_____

Your cake was _____.

Your guests received this party favor: _____

_____

_____

A highlight of your celebration was: _____

_____

_____

Quick mental snapshot: When I close my eyes, this is how I picture you: _____

_____

_____

Your nicknames are _____.

_____ are your best pals.

You're really into _____.

Funny thing YOU said recently . . .

exclusive
INTERVIEW

Conducted by _____ .

I met with _____ on _____
(CHILD'S NAME)   (DATE)

at our favorite spot,_____. My subject was dashing in

_____ and appeared quite _____
(ITEM OF CLOTHING WORN AT TIME)   (INTERESTED? BORED? HUNGRY?)

throughout the interview. We spoke on the record for about _____ minutes.

What were some of your favorite gifts that you got this year? _____

Tell me what immediately comes to mind when I say these words:

Home _____   Favorite color _____   Brother/sister _____

Magic _____   Bedtime _____   School _____

Hero _____   Cool _____   Love _____

What's the last thing you were sad about? _____

What makes you really *really* happy? _____

What do you look for in a friend? _____

_____

Are you scared of anything? _____

How does it feel to be in the double digits? _____

_____

Is there anything new that you think you should be allowed to do, now that you are one decade old?

_____

What do you think you'd like to be when you grow up? _____

Who's the last person you kissed? _____

_____

Your signature: _____

big
thoughts
from a not-so-little person

At what age is a person officially a grown-up? _____
_____
_____
_____
_____

What does mom or dad do at work all day? _____
_____
_____
_____
_____

If you could always get everything that you want, do you think you'd always be happy? _____
_____
_____
_____
_____

What do you think heaven is like? _____
_____
_____
_____
_____

time capsule
a present for
the future

— Year 10 —

Suggested items to tuck inside:

- Tenth birthday party invitation
- Tracing of your hand
- Piece of string as long as you are tall
- Sample artwork
- Newspaper clipping or printout of online news headlines
- A card that you wrote or received
- Report card or program from a school recital or play
- A quick note written by your decade-old self to your twenty-year-old, two-decade self
- Your birthday wish list on a folded-up piece of paper

Sealed on _____

by _____

11

you to the 11th power

Random pic from your
11th year on earth

11th BIRTHDAY

Your Big Day

We celebrated this birthday by: _____

A list of friends and family that joined the festivities: _____

_____

_____

Your cake was _____.

Your guests received this party favor: _____

_____

A highlight of your party was: _____

_____

_____

Quick mental snapshot: When I close my eyes, this is how I picture you: _____

_____

_____

Your nicknames are _____.

_____ are your best pals.

You're really into _____.

Funny thing YOU said recently . . .

exclusive
INTERVIEW

Conducted by _____.

I met with _____ on _____
(CHILD'S NAME)   (DATE)

at our favorite spot,_____. My subject was dashing in

_____ and appeared quite _____
(ITEM OF CLOTHING WORN AT TIME)   (INTERESTED? BORED? HUNGRY?)

throughout the interview. We spoke on the record for about _____ minutes.

What were some of your favorite gifts that you got this year? _____

Tell me what immediately comes to mind when I say these words:

Home _____ Favorite color _____ Brother/sister _____

Magic _____ Bedtime _____ School _____

Hero _____ Cool _____ Love _____

What's the last thing you were sad about? _____

What makes you really *really* happy? _____

What's your favorite smell? Least favorite? _____

If you could paint our house any color, what would it be? _____

What do you think you'd like to be when you grow up? _____

_____

Do you like your name? _____

Desert island questions: You get to bring one from each category with you.

Favorite music _____ Book _____ Movie _____

TV show _____ Computer game or play system game _____

Who's the last person you kissed? _____

Your signature: _____

TOP PRIORITIES

bonus
page

What's on your mind these days?
List the first five things that
pop into your head.

time capsule

a present for the future

──── Year 11 ────

Suggested items to tuck inside:

- Tracing of your hand
- Piece of string as long as you are tall
- Sample artwork
- Newspaper clipping or printout of online news headlines
- A card that you wrote or received
- Report card or program from a school recital or play
- Copy of a page from your mom's day planner or a handwritten summary of a typical day/week
- Your birthday wish list on a folded-up piece of paper

Sealed on _____

by _____

12

voilà, you. age 12

Random pic from your
12th year on earth

12th **BIRTHDAY**

Your Big Day

To make this day all about you, we decided to: _____

You hosted a group of V.I.P.s including: _____

_____

_____

Your special birthday dessert was: _____

Everyone walked away from the main event with: _____

_____

A highlight of your party was: _____

_____

_____

Quick mental snapshot: When I close my eyes, this is how I picture you: _____

_____

_____

Your nicknames are _____.

_____ are your best pals.

You're really into _____

_____.

Funny thing YOU said recently . . .

exclusive
INTERVIEW

Conducted by _____.

I met with _____ on _____
(CHILD'S NAME)   (DATE)

at our favorite spot,_____. My subject was dashing in

_____ and appeared quite _____
(ITEM OF CLOTHING WORN AT TIME)   (INTERESTED? BORED? HUNGRY?)

throughout the interview. We spoke on the record for about _____ minutes.

What were some of your favorite gifts that you got this year? _____

Tell me what immediately comes to mind when I say these words:

Home _____   Favorite color _____   Brother/sister _____

Magic _____   Bedtime _____   School _____

Hero _____   Cool _____   Braces_____   Love _____

What's the last thing you were sad about? _____

What makes you really *really* happy? _____

How do you feel about your last year as a preteen? _____

_____

Are there any toys or other kid stuff that you really don't want to give up yet? _____

_____

Complete this sentence: The one rule in my house I would change would be: _____

_____

In honor of being twelve . . . which of the following dozen would you most want:

⚪ dozen donuts   ⚪ dozen bagels   ⚪ dozen roses

Who's the last person you kissed? _____

Your signature: _____

we interrupt your regularly
scheduled birthday for this
SPECIAL MESSAGE

My Dearest _____,

I'm so honored to be your _____.

This is what I remember most about being your age: _____

_____

_____

_____

_____

If I could guarantee that you'd never get cavities or a stomach ache, I would give you buckets of candy, my

most favorite kind being: _____

_____

_____

_____

If I could give you one piece of advice, it would be this: _____

_____

_____

_____

May your twelfth year bring you joy, _____, and _____.

Love, _____

time capsule

a present for the future

— Year 12 —

Suggested items to tuck inside:

- Tracing of your hand
- Piece of string as long as you are tall
- Sample artwork
- Newspaper clipping or printout of online news headlines
- A card that you wrote or received
- Report card or program from a school recital or play
- A sample of your math homework
- Your birthday wish list on a folded-up piece of paper

Sealed on _____

by _____

13

NOW ENTERING: **the teen years**

Random pic from your
13th year on earth

13th **BIRTHDAY**

Your Big Day

We celebrated your new status by: _____

Your sophisticated list of invitees: _____
_____

Your special birthday dessert was: _____

Your guests walked away from the event with: _____
_____

A highlight of your party was: _____
_____
_____

Quick mental snapshot: When I close my eyes, this is how I picture you: _____
_____
_____

Your nicknames are _____.
_____ are your best pals.

You're really into _____.

Funny thing **YOU** said **recently . . .**

exclusive
INTERVIEW

Conducted by _____ .

I met with _____ on _____
         (CHILD'S NAME)   (DATE)

at our favorite spot, _____ . My subject was dashing in

_____ and appeared quite _____
         (ITEM OF CLOTHING WORN AT TIME)   (INTERESTED? BORED? HUNGRY?)

throughout the interview. We spoke on the record for about _____ minutes.

What were some of your favorite gifts that you got this year? _____

Tell me what immediately comes to mind when I say these words:

Home _____   Favorite color _____   Brother/sister _____

Magic _____   Bedtime _____   School _____

Hero _____   Cool _____   Love _____

What do you look for in a friend? _____

How do you think your best friends would describe you? _____

_____

What's the biggest life lesson you've learned thus far? _____

_____

What are your biggest fears? _____

What are your thoughts about God? _____

Do you like your name? _____

What's your most treasured item of clothing? _____

How do you feel about being a teenager? What are you most looking forward to about these teen years?

_____

Who's the last person you kissed? _____

Your signature: _____

a self-portrait
(or still life) by

_____

Grab a pen, pencil, marker, or pastel and take a moment to draw your teenage self or capture a corner of your bedroom. Don't worry about whether it's "good" or not. Art doesn't concern itself with that. Feel free to add written descriptions (like call-outs, captions, etc.) if you'd like.

time capsule

a present for the future

Year 13

Suggested items to tuck inside:

- Tracing of your hand
- Piece of string as long as you are tall
- Sample artwork or doodles
- Newspaper clipping or printout of online news headlines
- Report card or program from a school recital or play
- Your schedule for a typical day/week
- Your birthday wish on a folded-up piece of paper

Sealed on _____

by _____

14

it is with great pleasure that we present . . . you, age 14

Random pic from your
14th year on earth

14th **BIRTHDAY**

Your Big Day

You wanted to celebrate by: _____

Some people who made your day: _____
_____

Your dessert of choice: _____

Your guests walked away from the event with: _____
_____

A highlight of your party was: _____
_____
_____

Quick mental snapshot: When I close my eyes, this is how I picture you: _____
_____
_____

Your nicknames are _____.

_____ are your best pals.

You're really into _____
_____
_____.

Funny thing YOU said recently . . .

exclusive
INTERVIEW

Conducted by _____.

I met with _____ on _____
                      (CHILD'S NAME)   (DATE)

at our favorite spot, _____. My subject was dashing in

_____ and appeared quite _____
        (ITEM OF CLOTHING WORN AT TIME)   (INTERESTED? BORED? HUNGRY?)

throughout the interview. We spoke on the record for about _____ minutes.

What were some of your favorite gifts that you got this year? _____

Tell me what immediately comes to mind when I say these words:

Home _____   Favorite color _____   Brother/sister _____

Magic _____   Bedtime _____   High school _____

Hero _____   Cool _____   Love _____

What's the last thing you were sad about? _____

What makes you most happy? _____

What do you look for in a friend? _____

What's the best way to cheer someone up? _____

What are your biggest fears? _____

Do you like your name? _____

What's your most treasured item of clothing? _____

How is it being a freshman? Is it harder than you thought? How are the social pressures? _____

_____

What do you think you might be when you grow up? _____

Who's the last person you kissed? _____

Your signature: _____

big
thoughts from an
opinionated teenager

At what age is a person officially a grown-up? _____
_____
_____
_____
_____

What does mom or dad do at work all day? _____
_____
_____
_____
_____

If you could always get everything that you want, do you think you'd be forever happy? _____
_____
_____
_____
_____

Do you have any thoughts about the afterlife? _____
_____
_____
_____
_____

time capsule

a present for the future

Year 14

Suggested items to tuck inside:

- Tracing of your hand
- Piece of string as long as you are tall
- Sample artwork or doodles from a school notebook
- Newspaper clipping or printout of online news headlines
- Page from your favorite magazine
- Report card or program from a school recital or play
- A piece of high school math homework
- Your birthday wish on a folded-up piece of paper

Sealed on _____

by _____

15

high five x 3 = age 15

Random pic from your
15th year on earth

Your Big Day

You wanted to celebrate by: _____

Some people who made your day: _____
_____

Your dessert of choice: _____

Your guests walked away from the event with: _____
_____

A highlight of your celebration was: _____
_____
_____

Quick mental snapshot: When I close my eyes, this is how I picture you: _____
_____
_____

Your nicknames are _____.
_____ are your best pals.

You're really into _____
_____.

Funny thing YOU said recently . . .

exclusive
INTERVIEW

Conducted by _____.

I met with _____ on _____
                (CHILD'S NAME)   (DATE)

at our favorite spot, _____. My subject was dashing in

_____ and appeared quite _____
     (ITEM OF CLOTHING WORN AT TIME)   (INTERESTED? BORED? HUNGRY?)

throughout the interview. We spoke on the record for about _____ minutes.

What were some of your favorite gifts that you got this year? _____

Tell me what immediately comes to mind when I say these words:

Home _____ Favorite color _____ Brother/sister _____

Magic _____ Bedtime _____ Hero _____

Cool _____ High school _____ Driver's permit _____

Weekends _____ Love _____

What's the last thing you were sad about? _____

What makes you most happy? _____

What do you look for in a friend? _____

How do you feel about your hair? _____

Does anything stress you out? _____

What do you think you might be when you grow up? _____

Do you feel ready to start learning how to drive? _____

Describe your perfect Saturday night: _____

Describe your perfect Sunday afternoon: _____

Who's the last person you kissed? _____

Your signature: _____

bonus page

what was cool
then . . . and now

adult side

teenager side

Back in _____ when I was 15 . . .

Right now in _____

My favorite song was:

_____

My favorite song is:

_____

My favorite movie was:

_____

My favorite movie is:

_____

My favorite TV show was:

_____

My favorite TV show is:

_____

My favorite book was:

_____

My favorite book is:

_____

My favorite junk food was:

_____

My favorite junk food is:

_____

My hero was:

_____

My hero is:

_____

I communicated with friends via:

_____

I communicate with friends via:

_____

It was cool to wear:

_____

It's cool to wear:

_____

On weekends we hung out at:

_____

On weekends we hang out at:

_____

Hooking up meant:

_____

Hooking up means:

_____

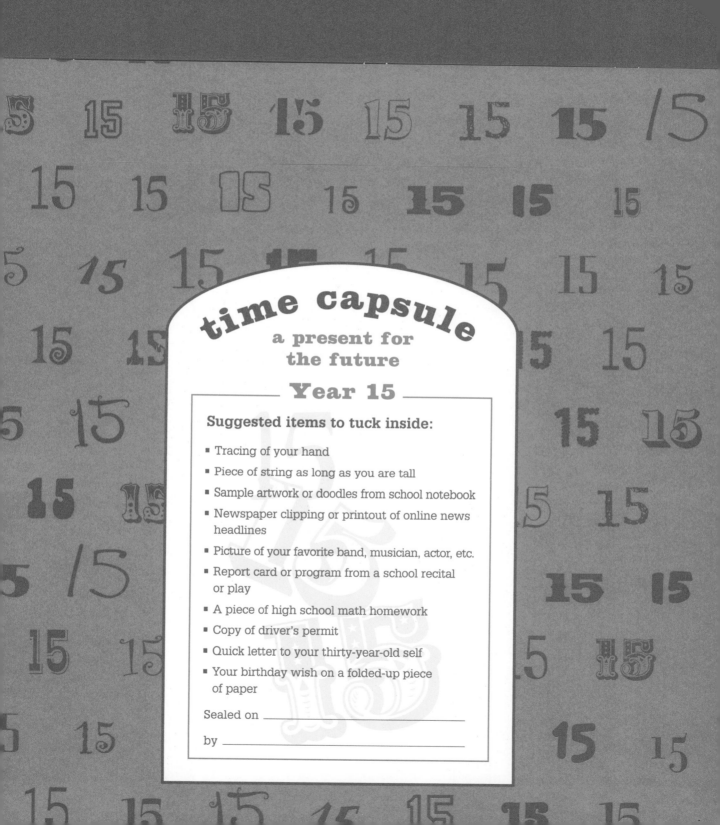

time capsule

a present for
the future

Year 15

Suggested items to tuck inside:

- Tracing of your hand
- Piece of string as long as you are tall
- Sample artwork or doodles from school notebook
- Newspaper clipping or printout of online news headlines
- Picture of your favorite band, musician, actor, etc.
- Report card or program from a school recital or play
- A piece of high school math homework
- Copy of driver's permit
- Quick letter to your thirty-year-old self
- Your birthday wish on a folded-up piece of paper

Sealed on _____

by _____

15 15 15 15 15 15
15 15 15 15 15 15 15
15 15 15 15 15 15 15 /5
15 15 15 15 15 15 15
15 15 15 15 15 15 15
15 15 15 15 15 15 15
15 15 15 15 15 15 15
15 15 15 15 15 15 15
15 /5 15 15 15 15 15
15 15 15 15 15 15 15
15 15 15 15 15 15 15

16

another sweet year

Random pic from your
16th year on earth

16th BIRTHDAY

Your Big Day

You wanted to celebrate by: _____

Some people who made your day: _____
_____

Your dessert of choice: _____
_____

A highlight of your celebration was: _____
_____
_____

Quick mental snapshot: When I close my eyes, this is how I picture you: _____
_____
_____

Your nicknames are _____.
_____ are your best pals.

You're really into _____
_____
_____.

Funny thing YOU said recently . . .

exclusive
INTERVIEW

Conducted by _____.

I met with _____ on _____
(CHILD'S NAME) (DATE)

at our favorite spot,_____. My subject was dashing in

_____ and appeared quite _____
(ITEM OF CLOTHING WORN AT TIME) (INTERESTED? BORED? HUNGRY?)

throughout the interview. We spoke on the record for about _____ minutes.

Favorite gifts? _____

Tell me what immediately comes to mind when I say these words:

Home _____ Favorite color _____ Brother/sister _____

Magic _____ Bedtime _____ Hero _____

Cool _____ High school _____ License! _____

Weekends _____ Curfew _____ Love _____

What's the last thing you were sad about? _____

What makes you most happy? _____

What do you look for in a friend? _____

What is your deepest fear? _____

Whose approach to life do you most admire, respect? _____

What would you like to be when you grow up? _____

Do you like your name? _____

Where do you plan to drive first? _____

Your dream car is? _____

Who's the last person you kissed? _____

Your signature: _____

teen $ $ CURRENCY

How much money do you make each month (through a job, allowance, etc.) _____
_____
_____
_____

How much do you try to save? _____
_____
_____
_____

Are you saving up for anything in particular? _____
_____
_____
_____

Do you keep an organized record of your spending/finances? _____
_____
_____
_____

Can you imagine being able to support yourself in the future? How much do you think this will cost per year?
_____
_____
_____
_____

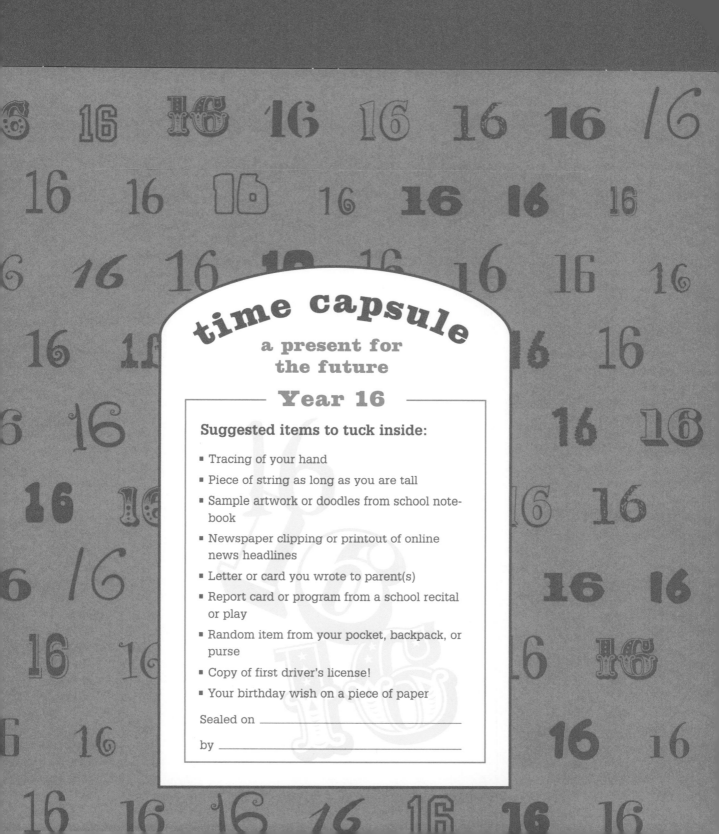

time capsule

a present for the future

Year 16

Suggested items to tuck inside:

- Tracing of your hand
- Piece of string as long as you are tall
- Sample artwork or doodles from school notebook
- Newspaper clipping or printout of online news headlines
- Letter or card you wrote to parent(s)
- Report card or program from a school recital or play
- Random item from your pocket, backpack, or purse
- Copy of first driver's license!
- Your birthday wish on a piece of paper

Sealed on _____

by _____

17

lo and behold . . . you!

Random pic from your
17th year on earth

th BIRTHDAY

Your Big Day

You wanted to celebrate by: _____

Some people who made your day: _____

_____

Your specially requested dessert: _____

A highlight of your celebration was: _____

_____

_____

Quick mental snapshot: When I close my eyes, this is how I picture you: _____

_____

_____

_____

Your nicknames are _____.

_____ are your best pals.

You're really into _____

_____

_____.

Funny thing YOU said recently . . .

exclusive
INTERVIEW

Conducted by _____.

I met with _____ on _____
                  (CHILD'S NAME)   (DATE)

at our favorite spot, _____. My subject was dashing in

_____ and appeared quite _____
  (ITEM OF CLOTHING WORN AT TIME)   (INTERESTED? BORED? HUNGRY?)

throughout the interview. We spoke on the record for about _____ minutes.

Favorite gifts? _____

Tell me what immediately comes to mind when I say these words:

Home _____ Favorite color _____ Brother/sister _____

Magic _____ Bedtime _____ Hero _____ Cool _____

High school _____ Job _____ Love _____

What's the last thing you were sad about? _____

What makes you most happy? _____

What do you look for in a friend? _____

Who do you idolize? What's the first thing you'd say to this person? _____

_____

Who brings out the very best in you? _____

_____

Where do you find spiritual fulfillment? _____

_____

What would you like to be when you grow up? _____

Who's the last person you kissed? _____

Your signature: _____

SLICE OF
life

bonus
page

Diagram your life in this handy pie-chart form. Fill in the slices with categories such as school, family, friends, activities, hobbies, jobs, or college prep. Big slices connote things that are the most important to you or that you spend the most time doing, and little slices are of course for the less significant, less time-consuming stuff. Add more slices or alter as you see fit.

time capsule

a present for the future

— Year 17 —

Suggested items to tuck inside:

- Tracing of your hand
- Piece of string as long as you are tall
- Newspaper clipping or printout of online news headlines
- Picture of your favorite band, musician, actor, sports figure, etc.
- Report card or program from a school recital or play
- Concert and/or movie ticket stubs
- Copy of a typical day from your school assignment book
- Your birthday wish on a folded-up piece of paper

Sealed on _____

by _____

18

you: officially an adult

Random pic from your
18th year on earth

18th **BIRTHDAY**

Your Big Day

We celebrated this significant day by: _____

Your guests of honor included: _____

_____

Your birthday dessert of choice: _____

A highlight of your celebration was: _____

_____

_____

Quick mental snapshot: When I close my eyes, this is how I picture you: _____

_____

_____

_____

_____

Your nicknames are _____.

_____ are your best pals.

You're really into _____

_____

_____.

Funny thing **YOU** said **recently . . .**

exclusive
INTERVIEW

Conducted by _____ .

I met with _____ on _____
(CHILD'S NAME)   (DATE)

at our favorite spot,_____ . My subject was dashing in

_____ and appeared quite _____
(ITEM OF CLOTHING WORN AT TIME)   (INTERESTED? BORED? HUNGRY?)

throughout the interview. We spoke on the record for about _____ minutes.

Favorite gifts? _____

Tell me what immediately comes to mind when I say these words:

Home _____ Brother/sister _____ Magic _____

Bedtime _____ Hero _____ Cool _____

High school _____ Graduation _____ College _____

Future_____ Childhood_____ Love_____

REPRISE Desert island questions: You get to bring one from each category with you.

Favorite music _____ Book _____ Movie _____

TV show _____ Computer game or play system game _____

What's the last thing you were sad about? _____

What makes you really *really* happy? _____

_____

What do you look for in a friend? _____

_____

Are you scared of anything? _____

_____

What are your thoughts about God? _____

_____

exclusive
INTERVIEW CONTINUED

What do you think you'd like to be when you grow up? _____
_____

Do you like your name? _____
_____

Have you registered to vote yet? Are politics important to you? _____
_____
_____

Describe your ideal road trip: _____
_____
_____

What memories come to mind about this book? Do certain years stand out? _____
_____
_____

Before we wrap this up, are there any questions you would like to ask ME? _____
_____
_____

How do you feel about ending this book? _____
_____
_____

Who's the last person you kissed? _____

Your signature: _____

time capsule

a present for the future

━━ Year 18 ━━

Suggested items to tuck inside:

- Graduation party invitation
- Tracing of your hand
- Piece of string as long as you are tall
- Sample artwork or doodles from school notebook
- Newspaper clipping or printout of online news headlines
- Report card or program from a school event
- Copy of a college admissions essay you wrote
- Copy of your first voter registration card
- Copy of your graduation diploma
- Copy of a college acceptance letter
- Your birthday wish on a folded-up piece of paper

Sealed on _____

by _____

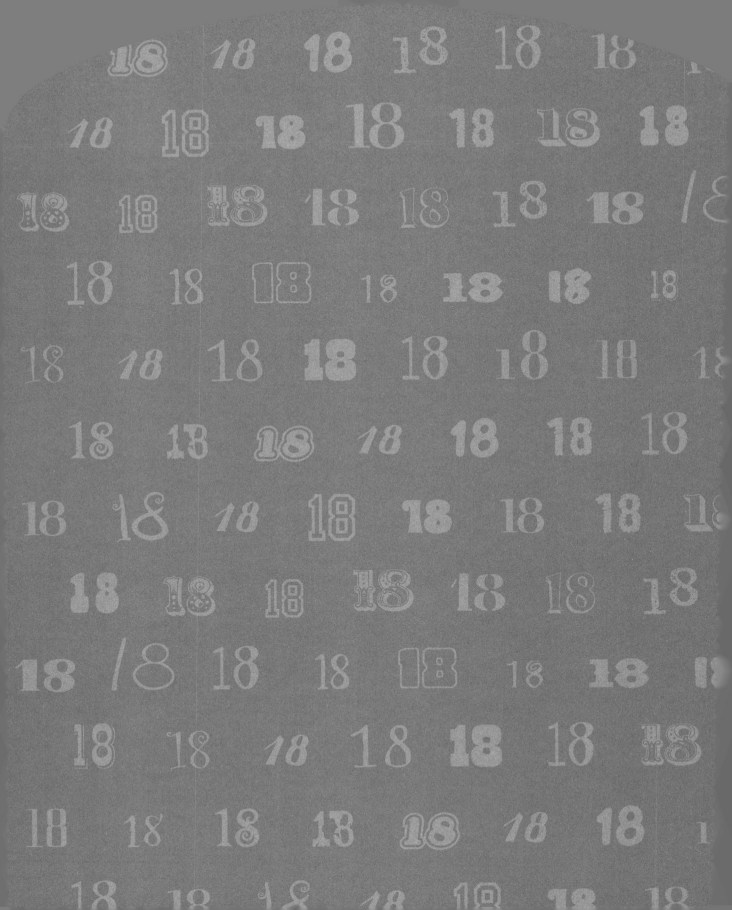

we started this at birth
we wrapped it up at eighteen
we've filled it out together
every year in between

HAPPY BIRTHDAY MY CHILD, MY YOUNG ADULT . . .

A special note to end this book: _____

_____

_____

_____

_____

_____

_____

_____

_____

_____

_____

_____

_____

_____

_____

_____

_____

_____

_____